THIS BOOK BELONGS

CHAPTERS:

1. "The Magical Star"   3
2. "Lucky's Curiosity"   5
3. "Exploring the Daytime World"   6
4. "Helping a Lost Little Girl"   16
5. "The Importance of Rest and Routine"   18
6. "The Power of a Child's Wish"   19
7. "Thankful for Experiences and Lessons"   20
8. "Lucky's Magical Gift to Children"   21

Chapter 1
The Magical Star

Once upon a time, high up in the sky, there lived a little magical star named Lucky. Her beautiful, wavy red hair was filled with twinkling and sparkling stars, and her eyes, like magical diamonds, could change color with her mood.

Lucky was very sweet and always made everyone happy with her kindness and friendly smile. She had a special gift - the magical power to make children's wishes come true and shine brightly in the night sky!

All day long, the little star peacefully rested and slept on soft, fluffy clouds in her cozy bed.

In this way, Lucky gathered positive energy from the sunlight and the gentle whispers of the wind. This energy gave her the strength not only to make all the children's dreams come true but also to shine in the night sky.

Chapter 2
Lucky's Curiosity

When night comes and Lucky lights up the stars in the sky, she becomes curious about what happens during the day while she sleeps. Lucky starts dreaming more about the secret world without darkness, imagining the sun's golden rays, nature's vibrant colors, and the joyful sounds all around. Excited by these dreams, she made a brave decision – to stay awake and see the wonders of the day with her own eyes!

Chapter 3
Exploring the Daytime World

In the morning, when the sun began to rise, Lucky decided to stay awake! She knew that stars are supposed to sleep during the day, but her curiosity about the daytime world was too strong. Lucky flew down from the sky on a white cloud and gently landed on the ground...

Little star was amazed by the beauty of the world and how everything was different in the daylight! The colors were bright and everything seemed more vibrant. She felt a sense of wonder and admiration she had never known before.

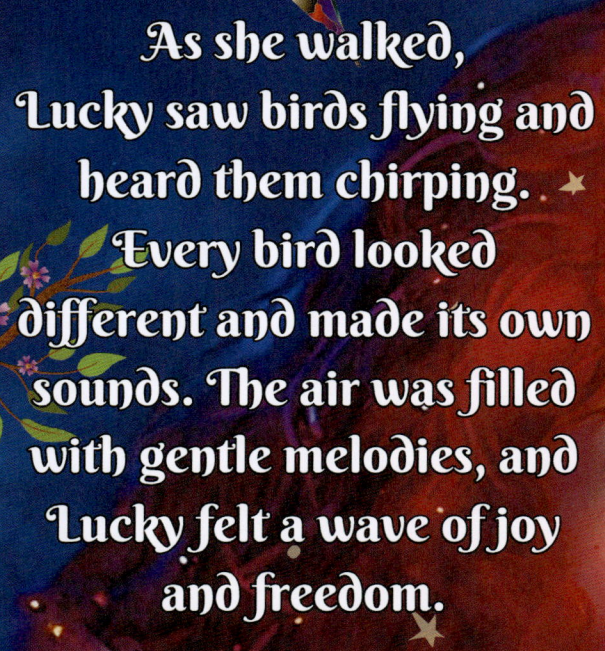

As she walked, Lucky saw birds flying and heard them chirping. Every bird looked different and made its own sounds. The air was filled with gentle melodies, and Lucky felt a wave of joy and freedom.

Soon, one bird landed on Lucky's hand. Touched by this unique feeling, she would always remember this moment! The birds reminded her of the simple pleasures of life, and the magical little star was grateful for the gift of seeing and hearing them.

Continuing her journey, Lucky saw a fantastic garden with an incredible smell that filled the air. Curious, she stepped inside and saw beautiful flowers blooming! Each flower was unique. Lucky wondered at how these colorful blossoms made life and beauty to everything around them.

With love, she gently touched the soft petals and enjoyed the sweet smells. The magical little star felt a sense of calm and peace wash over her. She realized that even the smallest things in nature can bring so much happiness and pleasure to the world around us.

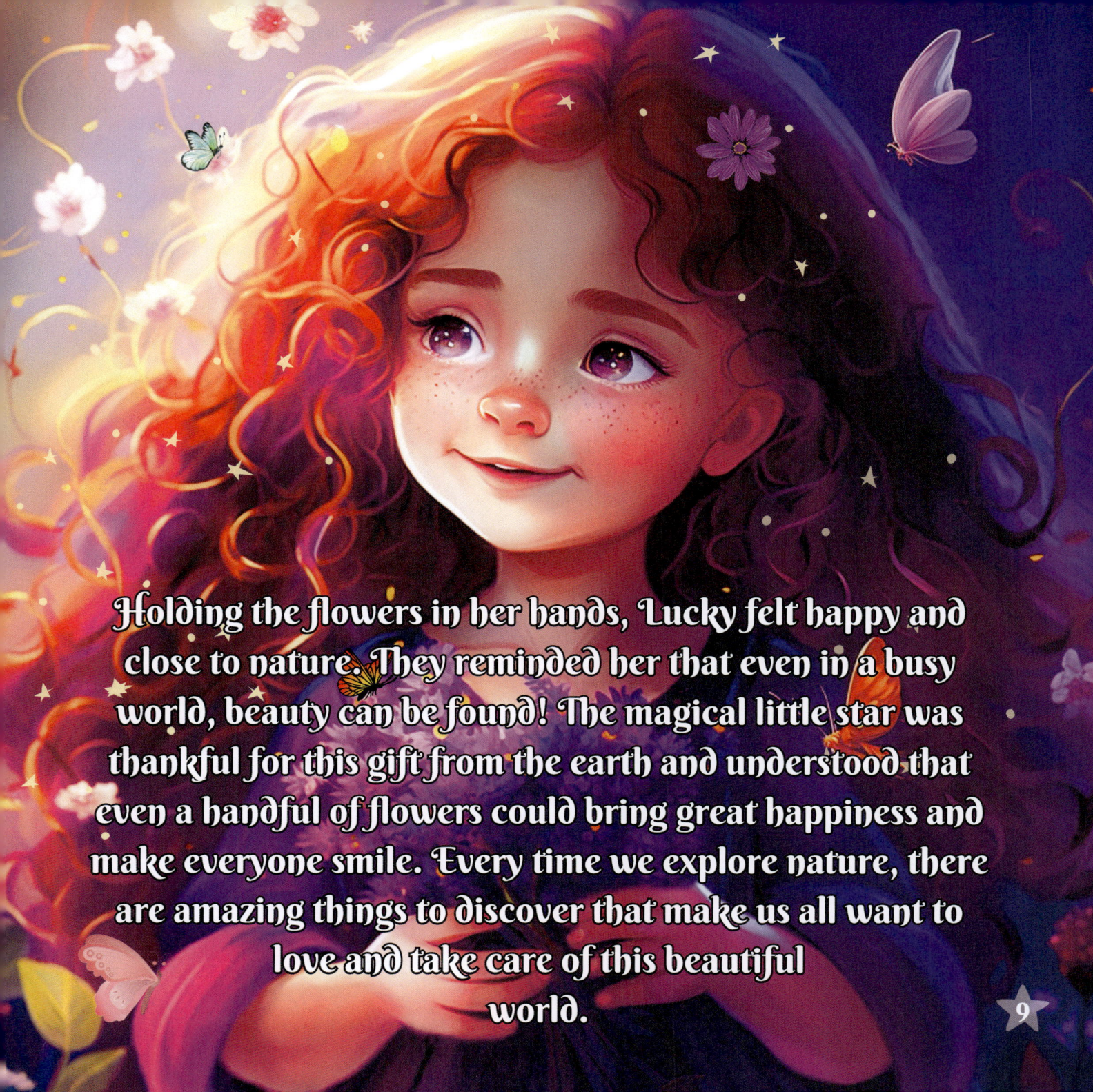

Holding the flowers in her hands, Lucky felt happy and close to nature. They reminded her that even in a busy world, beauty can be found! The magical little star was thankful for this gift from the earth and understood that even a handful of flowers could bring great happiness and make everyone smile. Every time we explore nature, there are amazing things to discover that make us all want to love and take care of this beautiful world.

Lucky continued her journey and came to the forest where the air was so fresh! The tall trees filled her with wonder, and she was warmly welcomed by lovely animals. Soon, a friendly bunny hopped in front of Lucky, charming her with its cute nose and soft tail.

A flock of colorful butterflies danced past, their wings sparkling in the sunshine. Lucky also saw playful squirrels in the trees, their fluffy tails swaying up and down, bringing a smile to Lucky's face. Then a majestic deer appeared and gracefully walked away. Each animal brought a new feeling of wonder and gratitude for the magical beauty of nature and the opportunity to be part of this wonderful world.

Little star visited the city and saw many tall buildings and busy streets full of cars and people. Lucky was amazed at how impressive life on the ground looked!

The buses and cars reminded her of big toys moving down the streets. She watched people rushing to work and doing their daily activities. The noise of the city was different from the peaceful life in the night sky, opening up a whole new world for Lucky, full of discoveries and adventures.

Later, Lucky lovingly watched children playing and running joyfully in the park. She was amazed by their energy! They seemed so carefree and happy! The magical little star saw families picnicking on the grass, laughing and talking, enjoying each other's company. The nearby peaceful fountain added to the wonderful atmosphere. It spread peace all around. Lucky also noticed dogs playing with people, wagging their tails and running after balls.

She admired the friendship between people and their pets! The little star had never experienced anything like it before, as everything on the ground was so different from the sky. Lucky felt a joyful curiosity, realizing there were so many new things on the ground to discover and enjoy.

Lucky continued her journey. The sun was shining brightly, and its warm rays filled her with happiness and energy. As she walked, she admired everything around her. Then dark clouds appeared in the sky, and a light rain began to fall. Lucky felt the soft drops on her skin and thought how pleasant and refreshing they were.

The soothing sound of rain falling on the leaves calmed her, and she enjoyed this new feeling. And then something magical happened! Lucky looked up and saw a colorful rainbow stretching across the sky. It was like a brightly colored bridge! The rainbow wasn't just beautiful, it completely amazed her.

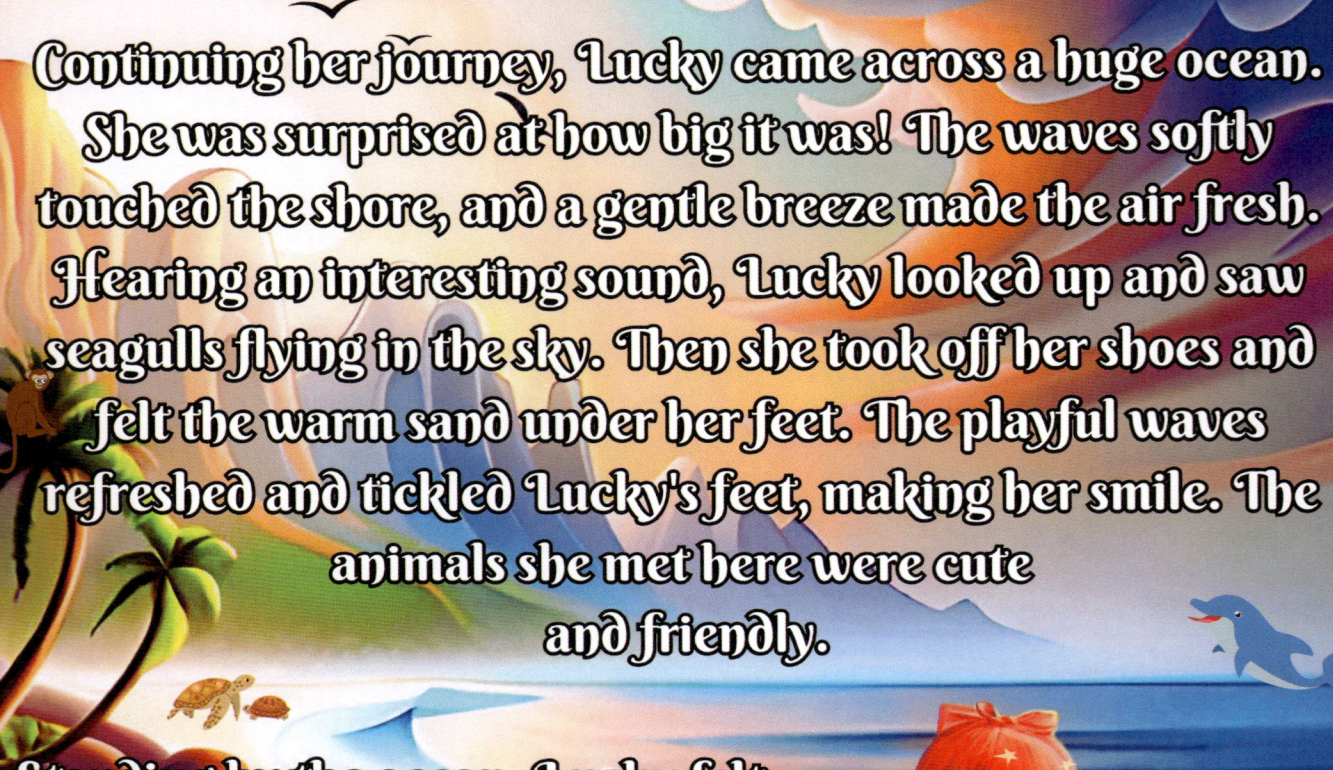

Continuing her journey, Lucky came across a huge ocean. She was surprised at how big it was! The waves softly touched the shore, and a gentle breeze made the air fresh. Hearing an interesting sound, Lucky looked up and saw seagulls flying in the sky. Then she took off her shoes and felt the warm sand under her feet. The playful waves refreshed and tickled Lucky's feet, making her smile. The animals she met here were cute and friendly.

Standing by the ocean, Lucky felt very calm. The rhythmic sound of the waves became a soft melody, and the sunset painted the sky with magical colors. Lucky treasured this spectacular moment by the ocean, adding it to her collection of unforgettable experiences.

Driven by curiosity, Lucky took a different path and climbed a hill. From there, she watched boats, ships, and yachts sailing in the water, and birds flying above them. Then she saw something incredible - an airplane flying in the sky!

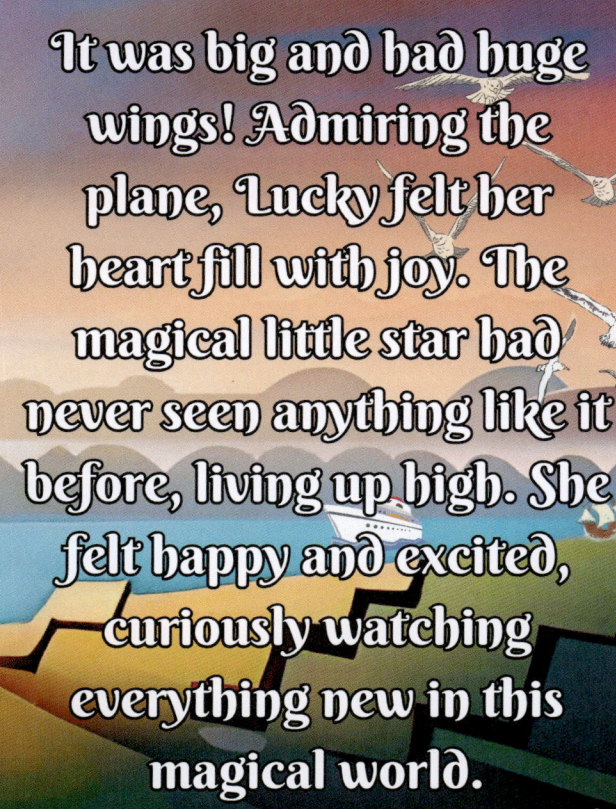

It was big and had huge wings! Admiring the plane, Lucky felt her heart fill with joy. The magical little star had never seen anything like it before, living up high. She felt happy and excited, curiously watching everything new in this magical world.

Chapter 4
Helping a Lost Little Girl

As the day went on, Lucky went to a small town. She walked until the sun started to go down. As the lights turned on all around, the streets and houses began to shine with a warm, magical glow. It created a cozy atmosphere and left an unforgettable impression on Lucky!

Suddenly, she saw a little girl alone and lost on the street. The girl was scared and crying because she couldn't find her way home. Feeling sad for the girl, the magical little star quickly wanted to help her.

Lucky's light sparkled, creating a shining path of stars in front of the little girl to follow. The girl's eyes widened with surprise as she saw the sparkling stars light up her way! Even in the darkest night, this special trail magically glowed.

Feeling happy and thankful for this wonderful help, the little girl took a brave step forward. With a smile on her face, she calmed and safely followed the star-path all the way back to her house. She would always remember this special night, keeping warm and magical memories in her heart forever, of when the stars showed her the way home.

Chapter 5
The Importance of Rest and Routine

Lucky felt very tired after staying up all day and walking a lot. Her light began to fade, and the stars that twinkled in her hair slowly disappeared. This taught Lucky the importance of rest for making wishes come true and lighting up the night sky.

After discovering interesting things on the ground, Lucky learned a lesson: rest and routine are important for everyone!

This way, she could have enough energy to make kids' dreams come true and light up the world. From this, Lucky learned that although adventures are fun and make life colorful, taking breaks is really important. Resting helps her feel strong again and ready to keep exploring, spreading light and happiness.

Chapter 6
The Power of a Child's Wish

The little boy wished with all his heart for a friend to play with, have adventures, and share fun moments.

Lucky's light was getting dim. She wanted to go home and rest, but then suddenly she heard a little boy whisper a wish!

Lucky was sleepy, but the little star knew she had to make the child's dream come true, as she does every night. Tired, Lucky wasn't sure if she could do it. However, the boy's wish filled her with the power to shine again and give him what he wanted.

Lucky, full of love, made the little boy's wish come true! She lit up the sky and filled the world with magic and beauty.

19

Chapter 7
Thankful for Experiences and Lessons

Living high in the sky, Lucky had never had so many adventures and different feelings as she did on the ground! She was thankful for her special life as a star and treasured every unforgettable moment she experienced while she was here. She knew these memories would stay with her forever!

Through this adventure, Lucky learned important lessons. She learned that getting enough rest makes her strong and helps her do important night jobs.

Lucky returned to the sky, full of love, gratitude, and joy, ready to continue spreading her light and bringing magic to all those who need it!

Chapter 8
Lucky's Magical Gift to Children

The little star has always felt grateful for her special gift - the magical power that makes her truly unique! With a heart full of love, Lucky waits every night as it is the time when she can make children's dreams come true.

Every time kids make a wish, Lucky listens carefully and is ready to make them happen, magically lighting up the night sky.

The sky comes alive as Lucky lights up the darkness with her magic, filling children's hearts with hope and making their dreams come true. She knows that every wish granted is a chance to make someone's world a little brighter and full of joy!

Look up at the sky, do you see the brightest star? That's Lucky! Every night, she shines brightly, helping to make your dreams come true!

THE END

Don't forget to make a wish

Lucky brightens our world with her magical light.

Now, close your eyes and whisper your wish to Lucky. She's always lovingly waiting to hear it!

Written by RegaSta

Dear Lovely Reader ★

Always be thankful for your unique talents, as they bring magic, joy, and happiness to you and those around you. Spread your kindness and love to others, and you will see how your warmth brightens their day, just like the stars light up the night sky. You have an incredible power to create the world a more beautiful
place!
Dream big, believe in yourself, and follow your heart. Just like Lucky - let your dreams take you on wonderful adventures and open up exciting possibilities, lighting up your future with happiness, success, and joy!
Also, remember what our magical friend learned: taking breaks is important too. With a heart full of love and a rested mind, you can follow your dreams and share your warmth everywhere you go.

My dear young reader, as you close this book, keep Lucky's spirit in your heart. You are a shining little star, so show your special light and shine brightly in the world around you! I hope your journey is filled with new amazing discoveries, fun adventures, wonders, and happy memories!

With love, light and dreams,
RegaSta

Printed in Great Britain
by Amazon